PETS

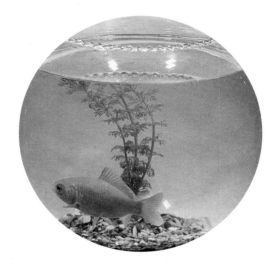

by Nicolas Thilo

Harcourt

Orlando   Boston   Dallas   Chicago   San Diego

Visit *The Learning Site!*

www.harcourtschool.com

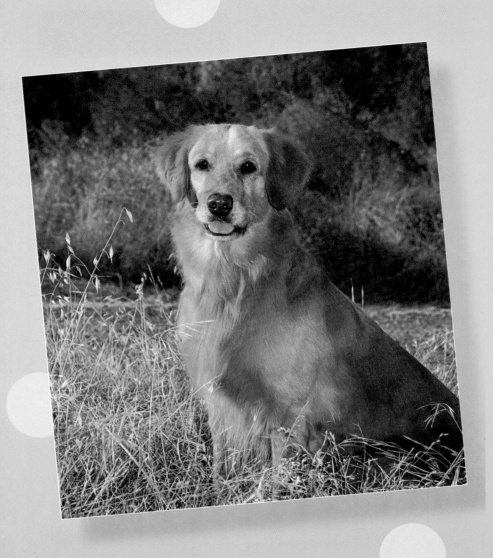

This is a dog.

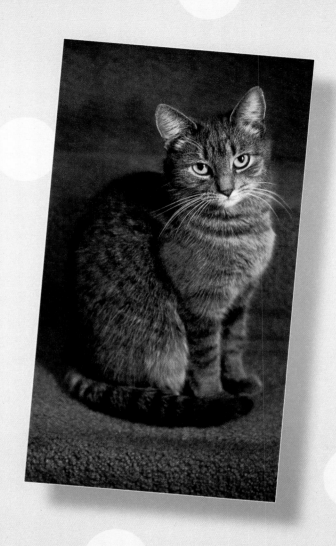

This is a cat.

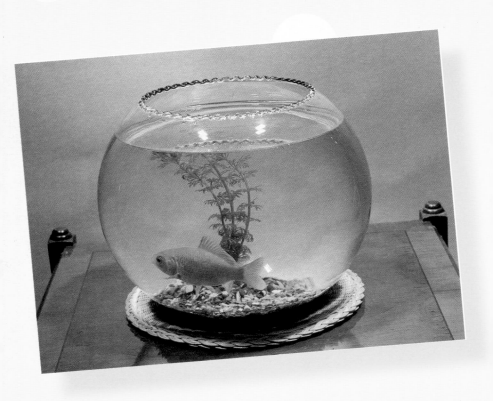

This is a fish.

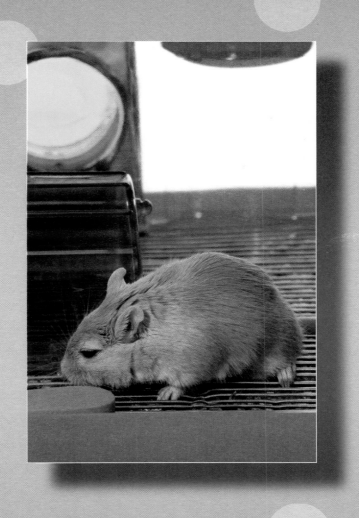

This is a gerbil.

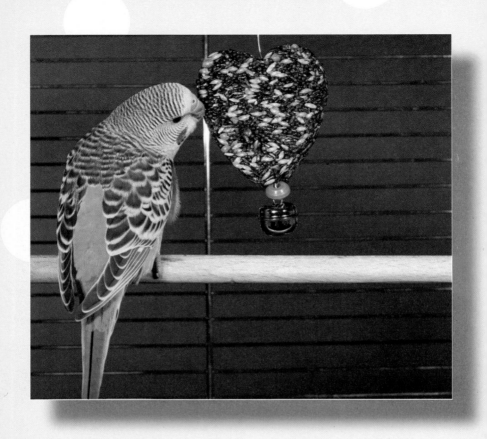

This is a bird.

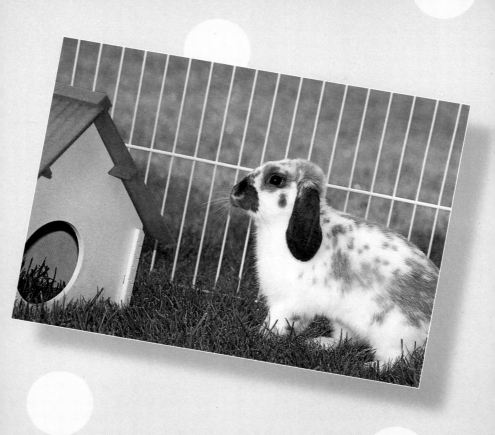

This is a rabbit.

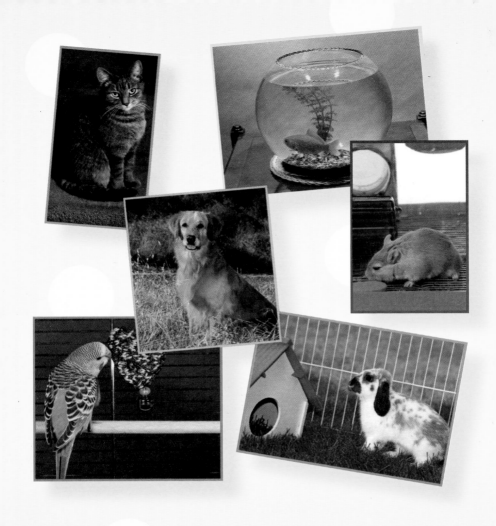

Do you like pets?